Let's Romp
in the Field of Words

Oddities and Audities
Snickers and Sound Traps
Coinages and Loose Broads — Oh My!

Sheldon Harper

LET'S ROMP IN THE FIELD OF WORDS
Oddities and Audities, Snickers and Sound Traps,
Coinages and Loose Broads—Oh My!

No part of this book may be reproduced or transmitted in any form or by any means, electronic or mechanical, including photocopying, recording, or by an information storage or retrieval system, now known or hereafter invented—except by a reviewer who may quote brief passages in a review to be printed online or in a magazine or newspaper—without permission in writing from the publisher.

For further information, contact the publisher:

Harper Ink
17322 Otani Court
Strongsville, OH 44136

Email: harperinkpress@gmail.com

The author has made every diligent effort to ensure that the information in this book is accurate. He assumes no responsibility for errors or omissions that are inadvertent or inaccurate. The views and opinions expressed in this book are not intended to endorse any product or person.

Copyright © 2011 Sheldon Harper
All rights reserved.

ISBN-10: 0615438571
EAN-13: 9780615438573

*Dedicated to the memory of Nita
and the presence of Claudia*

SAYS WHO?

(Also see back cover)

Harper not only stretches your imagination, he trowels out chuckles along the way as he exposes the humor that lurks behind even serious expressions. Try to avoid "twistophobia" as you sample the freakishness of many of the words we live by.

> – *Paul Bohn—author,* A Charging Rhino Would Make Your Heart Sing, *newspaper reporter, and former NASA public information director*

Sheldon Harper uses language playfully to educate, entertain, and delight his reader. *Let's Romp in the Field of Words* is a treat for all.

> – *Jan Sixt—private tutor and educator for 41 years and inductee into* Who's Who Among American Teachers

I could make an interesting speech on many of the words in this book. It's different. It's great!

> – *Clinton Friedley—speaker, language devotee, and author of acclaimed books on writing and grammar*

CONTENTS

   1   Thanks
   3   To Start With

   5   **The Playful Part**

   7   Oddities
 17   Audities
 23   There Oughta Be a Morphy's Law
 27   You Have My Word for It
 37   What a Fix We've Gotten Ourselves Into!
 41   Word Weeds
 45   American English Enlivens "Dead"
 49   Help!
 53   Breaking Your Word
 55   Opposites
 71   Man Handling
 73   Pluralsy
 75   Snickers
 83   Watch Out for Loose Broads
 85   Sound Traps
 91   Hey Webster . . .
 95   Namedroppings
 99   Nice (and otherwise) Sounds

103   **The Picky Part**

105   Of-alanche
111   When You Have the Floor . . .
115   Troublemakers
117   T.I.C. Grammar Rules
119   Want to Play Editor?

THANKS

My daughter, Shelley Hussey, author of ***I'm Not OK, You're Not OK, But That's OK With God***, gets my thanks and appreciation for navigating our trip through the tricky (by my standards) currents of publishing and its related technology. I thank her for digging her spurs into me—though not hard enough to draw blood—for rapping my knuckles, and for holding my hand.

To my steady, Claudia (AKA Madge) Lee, I give my thanks for her page-by-page inspection and perceptive comments. I won't admit, however, that she often beats me at anagrams and other word games.

Clinton Friedley—author, speaker, and noted teacher of grammar and writing—gave me *you-can-and-should-do-this* confidence.

Paul Bohn, former public relations guy at NASA, was encouraging and also an example of persistence as he published his own book.

At various times, my family and many others provided support, advice, and critiques as the words came together. They include Jeff Lee, who moved to Cleveland from California for, among other reasons, the weather (honest, that's what he said). And Ann Crawford, now of Frenchton, West Virginia, with whom I'm proud to share an ancestral tree. And Merritt Johnquest, Lou Amer, Lee Barthelman, Don Riethmiller, and George Brown of our northern Ohio ROMEO group (Retired Old Men Eating Out). And two savvy Jans: Bergkessel of Erie, Pennsylvania, and Sixt of Avon Lake, Ohio.

TO START WITH

My friend Merritt calls me a word freak. I plead guilty to this charge from a master of the language. He's been a friend since our 1950s and 1960s advertising days in Cleveland.

Here is an assembly, in no particular sequence, of notes and clippings about one of my favorite subjects, accumulated over many years. These words about words show the FREAKISH nature of our language: Funny, Rambling, Exasperating, Ambivalent, Kooky, Inconsistent, Sloppy, Haphazard. It's served in small bites for easy digestion. I hope you enjoy the taste.

Keep in mind that immigrants are expected to cope with this stuff. Heck, even people like you and I stumble often, and we got decent grades in elementary English, didn't we? So let's be patient with José, Olga, Gerhard, Liu, Sven, Baktar, Yvette, Stash, Antonio, and others—even "fluent" natives like those of us who grew up with the language but still tinker with it to get it right.

This is a put-down piece. You can put it down and not worry about forgetting the story line or a thickening plot, since neither exists. It's not even complete, because you (and maybe a friend you lend it to) probably can't resist the temptation to add to it. If you have comments, I'd like to hear from you.

Marilyn vos Savant, the Parade magazine columnist whose IQ is billed as the world's highest, says that English has the most words—a quarter-million or so—of any of the world's thousands of languages. That's quite a landscape to play around in.

Let's romp.

Sheldon Harper
Email: harperlee80@wowway.com

THE PLAYFUL PART

ODDITIES

Whether I deduct or deduce, it's a deduction.

* * *

Canny and uncanny aren't related. Neither are crease and increase, abuse and disabuse, meteors and meteorology, hearse and rehearse, brace and embrace, shorthand and shorthanded, curator and cure, posteriors and posterity, serve and deserve, ponder and ponderous. Many potholes litter the road to English fluency.

* * *

Hafner flied (not flew) out to center. Furcal flew (not flied) from first to third. Hafner used a bat. Furcal used his feet. There's a lot of wingless flying going on in baseball.

* * *

A high school or college wrestler scores a "tech (technical) fall" if his winning margin during the match reaches 15 points, ending the match. But his opponent is never tech fallen or tech fell, he's tech falled.

* * *

I don't see why the word queue needs those four vowels when its first letter says it all. I don't think we improved forecastle when we traded four of its letters for two apostrophes to make it a fo'c'sle.

* * *

ODDITIES

There's nothing casual about a casualty. Nor is there anything funny about a funny feeling or a brouhaha.

* * *

Until a longer one appears, I'll allow this claim: Longest vowel-less word is "tsktsks," which has seven consonants in a row. So does "rhythms" if you allow y as a consonant. Longest line of consecutive vowels? I saw five of 'em queueing up.

* * *

The winner of a gubernatorial race can't gubern and won't be a gubernor.

* * *

"To the contrary notwithstanding" sure is a cumbersome way to say "despite."

* * *

Flop flips: An outstanding event doesn't outstand, it stands out. And outcry is somewhat like cry out, as is outset to set out. But outtake doesn't relate to takeout, nor outlay to layout, or outwork to workout, or outlook to lookout, or outcome to come out. Moral: keep your syllables in the right order; unless you don't care if you oversleep on your sleepover.

* * *

Add an i to the one-syllable "smile" and it becomes the three-syllable "simile." That's a lot of power for one letter. Talk about power, one measly apostrophe can change both the sound and the meaning of were (we're) and wont (won't).

* * *

The difference between a wigwam and a tepee is roughly the difference between a wig and a toupee. Fitting.

* * *

The Titanic sank beneath the sea, but fish swim in the sea. Cables are laid under ground, but bodies are buried in the ground. On the surface, we seem not to have a deep understanding of depths.

* * *

Illogically, "midnight" and "the middle of the night" are quite different times.

* * *

"Unbeknownst" should defer to the simpler and shorter "unknown," allowing that dated word to join amongst and whilst in retirement.

* * *

If you know a contemptible good old boy, you know a double oxymoron.

* * *

The infantry isn't for infants, who are at home in a nursery, which isn't a home for nurses. Is it now becoming clearer why immigrants take a while to learn English?

* * *

The word indict should rhyme with predict, but it rhymes (without reason) with invite.

* * *

You can't see a radio show or dial a press tab phone. Your cruise ship sails without sails.

* * *

You can't identify any of the four corners of the earth, but there are four corners in the misnamed boxing ring.

* * *

You sign in ink, which seems to explain why an omen-type sign is an inkling.

* * *

The word penmanship surely won't live much longer. It describes a fading art, and its middle syllable is sexist.

* * *

"Well I'll be . . ." is a partial sentence but a complete thought.

* * *

The word "usher" contains four personal pronouns in order: us, she, he, her. I can't take credit for this momentous discovery . . . I read it somewhere.

* * *

This may be our wildest verbiage: To rouse Jim you can awake, awaken, wake, or waken him. You have then awaked, awakened, awoke, awoken, waked, wakened, woke, or woken him. And that's before we get to the uppers: wake up, wakened up, waked up, woke up, woken up. Your options may seem intimidating, but I'd not lose a lot of sleep over it. Think of it as the English language at play.

* * *

You can blame the weather for some language aberrations. It can be summery but not wintery (wintry, if you please). We can feel the warmth but not the coldth. Climatology is the study of climate, but the study of weather is not weatherology; it's meteorology, which has little if anything to do with meteors. Don't blame me; I just report this stuff.

* * *

We're swamped with spellings of certain sounds. For example, the "oo" sound in the word boo is also in two, rue, dew, Sioux, coup, lulu, who, through, beauty, rendezvous, adieu, and plain old ooh.

* * *

Salve has not only two sounds but also two meanings. To salve (rhyme with valve) is to salvage. A salve (rhyme with have) is an ointment. When you halve an orange you have two halves but you shouldn't pronounce the l's, as you would in valve, which has no vave. I'm beginning to regret bringing this up.

* * *

Here are some pronunciation-challenged interlopers: the breathy phew and whew, the no-vowels Btfsplk (Joe, the Al Capp character in "L'il Abner"), and the profane #%$&% #&$, which has a zillion spellings.

* * *

Ed often works in disguise, losing his identity as he moves between one- and two-syllable words that appear similar. He became a blessed (bless-ed) person after he was blessed (blest). He's a two-legged (legg-ed) batter who legged (leggd) it to first base. He crooked (crookd) his crooked (crook-ed) finger. He dogged (doggd) his quarry with dogged (dogg-ed) determination. His grandpa is an aged (age-ed) person who aged (agd) gracefully. His aim was off as he only winged (wingd) the two-winged (wing-ed) duck. However, stooped is never stoop-ed because that would be stupid.

* * *

David Jacquet, ("The Straight Jacquet"), points out that the word "once" can refer to the past, the present, or the future: "I once lived in Iowa" ... "Do it at once" ... "Once you take this pill, you'll feel better."

* * *

Fourth, fifth, sixth, seventh, eighth, and ninth hold to the "th" ending. But first, second, and third allow us to avoid oneth, twoth, and threeth. And we have forty, fifty, sixty, seventy, eighty, and ninety with the "ty" tag, but there's no onety, twoty, or threety. We should probably be grateful for this merciful pattern-breaking.

* * *

A newspaper story tells us that 381 words are in our dictionaries because of typographical errors or misreadings. The guilty words weren't listed, but it probably doesn't matter since the statute of limitations has surely expired.

* * *

Some questions are really suggestions or offers, such as "Why don't you pick up the mail on your way home?" and

ODDITIES

"Why not stop by some time?" Requiring no response are these questions-that-aren't: "What can I say," "What'll they think of next," "Ain't it the truth," "Wouldn't you know it," "Who would have thought," and the sales pitch "Why pay shipping."

* * *

Soft relates to softly. But does hard have a similar relative? Hardly.

* * *

When you hear the term "pretender to the throne" don't you wonder why pretense qualifies anyone to sit that high? And don't you wonder how long doctors and lawyers have to practice before they're ready for the real thing?

* * *

Your statement "I didn't see him fall" has five different meanings, based on which word you emphasize. Stressing the I means you didn't see him fall, but someone else might have. Your DIDN'T means you deny seeing him fall. You didn't SEE him fall, but you heard the sound (ouch). You didn't see HIM fall, but you saw someone else fall. And you didn't see him FALL, but you saw him teeter.

* * *

If you can't decide whether he has a hair-trigger temper, a short temper, a quick temper, a bad temper, or just a temper, you can temporize with "low boiling point."

* * *

The past tense of the verb lead (leed) is led, which is also the metallic noun lead (led). The past tense of read (reed) is read (red), and both reed and red are words with different meanings. As I re-read this, it seems silly and confusing. You should probably just ignore it and go on to the next one.

* * *

"There is a peculiar fascination in other people's tragedy that is very universal to man" is a quote from a newspaper story. Does "very universal" describe a greater degree than a simple "universal"? No. Just the opposite. By modifying universal, the word "very" suggests a scale. In reaching for superlatives when none is required, we sap word strength.

* * *

"I have every confidence we'll find a good temporary solution," said a BP spokesman about the Gulf oil gusher. He didn't say how many confidences were available, but if he's got all of 'em, I guess that's good to know.

* * *

A triumph is a win. So when an orchestra completes a triumphant tour, who loses?

* * *

A clerical job doesn't require a cleric, and a racy movie isn't necessarily about racing or ethnicity.

* * *

A newspaper headline said that "Women and minorities are a fraction of firm partners," leaving unanswered the question of large or small fraction. There's so much room between one-hundredth and ninety-nine hundredths, for example, that "fraction" seems hardly sufficient to cover both.

* * *

All pronouns refer to someone or something specific. At least that's what they say.

* * *

As a country roads kid I often wore overhauls. I learned later that city people called 'em overalls. Actually, both describe the same thing.

* * *

Is it pigeon or pidgeon? To d or not to d is the question. Repeat after me: smidgeon, bludgeon, and curmudgeon have a d, but surgeon, sturgeon, and pigeon don't (deceased actor Walter Pidgeon to the contrary).

* * *

"He has a temperature," "I wish you luck," "there's a guy with character," "she's a woman with a reputation," "today's kids have an attitude," "a person with morals." High or low temperature? Good or bad luck? What kind of character? Reputation for what? What kind of attitude? Usually you know the meaning in each case because in today's discourse the operative noun usually carries its own negative or positive cachet.

* * *

"Take it easy" is a versatile term. It can mean "simmer down" or "watch your step" or "don't overdo it" or "be careful with that" or "don't be rough on him" and probably more. It's a useful injunction when you don't want to (or can't) be more specific.

* * *

Being beaten up is bad enough, but being beaten down is a real downer.

※ ※ ※

Leapt and leaped are both legit, as are dreampt and dreamed, and burnt and burned. But crept has no creeped, dealt has no dealed, wept has no weeped. Conversely, the "eds" prevail in cropped (no cropt), and chipped (no chipt), and flipped and flopped have no flipt or flopt. No doubt there are many more of these, but I stopped researching because I got too tensed.

※ ※ ※

These words differ slightly in their definitions, but I hope you don't ask me what they are: adage, aphorism, bon mot (or just mot), catchword, dictum, epigram, maxim, old saw (and just saw), precept, and proverb . . . plus others I ran across as I checked my Roget: apothegm, gnome, and scholium. Confronted with this intimidating selection, I often settle for just sayin' "saying."

AUDITIES

Many "sn-" words have to do with the nose: snore, snort, sniff, snoot, snoop, sneeze, sniffle, snivel, snuff. It's an audity, but maybe it snot significant.

* * *

One sound, four different words and meanings: ore, oar, or, o'er . . . aisle, I'll, ile, eye'll. And there's at least one sound that sneaks into seven words—the "ood" in sued, food, who'd, lewd, brewed, you'd, and dude. Many spellings are also guilty of fickle behavior, like the "omb" that changes its sound from tomb to bomb to comb to aplomb.

* * *

I tried to find an "-ash" word that doesn't rhyme with lash, mash, splash, cash, bash, dash, clash, trash, smash, flash, brash, etc., but I couldn't, so I finally had to wash my hands of the whole thing.

* * *

After much research, I reported to Claudia that all "-ays" words rhyme: bays, days, jays, pays, rays, and so on. Her response: "Says who?"

* * *

The letter w is unpredictable. It's sounded but not written in "one," "once," "oui," and "Ouija board." It's written but not sounded in "two," "whole," "sword," and "answer."

And it's the only letter with more than one syllable when you pronounce it.

* * *

Note the pronunciation changes, in both letters and syllables, that one letter can cause: Put a y at the end of crochet and croSHAY becomes CROTCHety. An o following concert changes CONsert to conCHAIRtoe. Replace Quixote's e with ic and keeOHtay becomes quixAHtic. And you don't sound the g in malign until it becomes malignant.

* * *

Moving right along, the t's in soften and ballet aren't heard until they become softer and balletic. You don't say the p in coup unless you put a re in front. The letter b is ignored in dumber and plumber, gets attention in lumber and cucumber, and gets it both ways in number, depending on whether you're talking about a numeral or a degree of numbness.

* * *

We write "victuals" but say "vittles." It's spelled "Worcester" (Massachusetts) but spoken "Wooster," for which we might blame the English, but it was their town first, and with a "shire" on the end. Ohio avoids the problem with its Wooster by spelling it that way.

* * *

When south becomes southern, two sounds change: the ou and the th. Add er to moth, both, and broth, and an e to cloth and breath, and you again change both the vowel sounds and the th sounds in each word.

* * *

You could say—but you probably won't, so I will—that appreciation for Jean in jeans was built into Gene's genes.

* * *

Nature is "NAY-cher" but mature is "ma-TOOR," which seems unNATchural.

* * *

The sounds of the Chicago Children's Chorus are inconsistent because the three Ch's have different pronunciations: sh, ch, and k. It comes out Shicago Children's Korus.

* * *

When a woman becomes plural, she changes the pronunciation but not the spelling of the first syllable, and changes the spelling but not the unaccented sound of the second syllable. If you disapprove, *you* tell her.

* * *

Leo isn't dependable. He sounds his o in Leon and leotard, but not in leopard or Leonard.

* * *

Prelude is pronounced prelyude, prelood, praylude, or preelude. You hear amateur as amater, amatyour, or amacher. With English you get choices.

* * *

You should sound the s's in Des Plaines but not the ones in Des Moines. It's strange that Illinois and Iowa can't agree on their towns' s's, since they share four of them in their common-border river name.

* * *

AUDITIES

It's an arch in archdeacon but an ark in archaeology. The architect of this confusion is my archenemy.

* * *

Can you explain to your Martian visitor why laughter doesn't rhyme with daughter? Why the bris in debris doesn't rhyme with the one in hubris? Why colonel and kernel are aurally one? Why mouth, vermouth, and Plymouth have three different "mouth" sounds? Why broach is a pronunciation for brooch? Good luck.

* * *

Motorcade, brocade, arcade, and cavalcade agree on the pronunciation of their cade. But then comes façade, a French word. Wouldn't you know it.

* * *

English language learners must go nuts with the –ose and –oose words. Chose and choose should match lose and loose in rhyme and pronunciation, right? And since chose is the past tense of choose, lose would be the past tense of loose, right? Su-u-u-r-r-r-e.

* * *

Hard g's go soft from dangle to danger, angle to angel, and Angola to Angela. They often make the same change within a word: baggage, gorgeous, gauge, Gidget. Now I'm looking for a word that has both the hard and soft sounds *together* in its double g. Can you suggest one?

* * *

LLOYD LLEWELLYN has LLAMAS on his LLANO, but you'll never see LLIONS on LLAWRENCE LLAWSON'S LLAWN.

* * *

Y'know what happened to those t sounds that left moist, fast, and haste when the words became moisten, fasten, and hasten? They sneaked soundlessly in front of (t)sunami, (t)setse, and (t)sar.

* * *

The letter p may be the shyest letter. It hides its sound in all those pneum- words like pneumonia; in the psi-s, psy-s, and pseudo-s; and in birds like ptarmigans and the pterodactyl that King Kong fought. It also joins h to sound like an f in Philadelphia and the phon-, phen-, and phar- words. Although there is no Fantom of the Opera, phantasy is legit as a variant of fantasy (just as phrenetic and frenetic are interchangeable), demonstrating again that p is phickle and phrivolous. It's so conphusing. Fooey on such fonetics.

* * *

The "mn" letter pair is an m sound in hymn, solemn, and many other words, but has an n sound in the only word it begins: mnemonics. Can you remember that?

* * *

I see the word Yosemite and I want to say YOSE-mite, not Yo-SEM-it-e, for the same reason I say DY-namite instead of dy-NAM-it-e. And when I look at hyperbole and calliope, my impulse is to say HY-per-bole and CAL-i-ope instead of the proper hy-PER-bol-e and ca-LI-o-pe. Do you have such urges?

* * *

"On" often sounds like "un": ton, wonder, honey, money, done, none, won, London, sponge, Monday. It can also rhyme with "own": lone, bone, hone, phone, pone, pony, Sony, prone. You could say it's an unsound sound.

* * *

Some of our soundalike words are, as you would expect, related, as in these pairs: residents/residence, correspondents/correspondence, incidents/incidence, and silents/silence. But there's no kinship in patience/patients or presence/presents.

* * *

Trivia question: What do these words have in common: subject, contest, combine, produce, contrast, insult, object, protest, record? Answer: As nouns, their accent is on the first syllable; but as verbs, the accent shifts to the second syllable. If you know of a rule at work here, I hope you'll tell me.

THERE OUGHTA BE A MORPHY'S LAW

When words morph into different parts of speech, some seem to follow no rules. We need a Morphy's Law to keep order. Just look at this mess:

Past tenses of the non-rhyming verbs work, seek, buy, and fight, are the rhyming wrought (as in "What hath God wrought?"), sought, bought, fought. Conversely, the rhyming verbs fight, light, and sight become non-rhyming fought, lit, and sighted. Somehow, we must keep such way-word behavior from spreading!

* * *

Beast and feast become bestial and festive, losing a's (and rationality?) in the process. When solve and serve go to resolve and reserve, their s sounds go to z sounds, and the re changes the meanings entirely. The noun forms of relieve and believe are relief and belief. But deceive and receive opt for deception and reception. Standards, anyone?

* * *

Ferocious has ferocity, but delicious has no delicity. Win has a won but no winned, and sin has a sinned but no son (to save us from our word sins).

* * *

I don't know why star needs a dumb adjective like stellar when it can slide so smoothly into starry or starlike, for heaven's sake.

* * *

Some proper nouns appear to morph improperly. You're Gallic if you're from France, and Hellenic if you live in Greece. A devotee of George Bernard Shaw is a Shavian. Jupiter is Jovian. A resident of Liverpool (the one in England) is a Liverpudlian (from pool to puddles?), and the natives of Glasgow (Scotland) are Glaswegians. But—although Filipinos come from The Philippines and Muscovites from Moscow—we still see no sign of blood from a turnip.

* * *

Rarefy converts its e to an i when it goes to rarity, as does liquefy when it turns into liquid. Both without approval, as far as I know.

* * *

Consider the strange case of the four aces. Race and face become racial and facial, but space and palace reject their c's in favor of t's as they turn into spatial and palatial.

* * *

You just can't be too careful with all this morph-deception going on. The ai in sustain and maintain turns into a simple e in sustenance and maintenance. Pronounce, announce, and renounce lose their second syllable o's as they become pronunciation, annunciation, and renunciation. Appeal and reveal lose a's en route to appellate and revelation. It's scandalous.

* * *

Once in a while a word evolves, slowly and without fanfare, into a new identity. Depending on what crowd you hang with, you've probably heard "Jesus Christ" as profanity, sometimes with a mysterious middle initial H. At some point the term was shortened to Jesus. Then, as a modicum of religious sensitivity began to assert itself, you often heard jeez, which slid into sheesh. Sheese!

YOU HAVE MY WORD FOR IT

Sometimes you can't think of the word you want—one that expresses your thoughts exactly. You may decide it just doesn't exist. Why not invent it? Here I propose some new words for your consideration, followed by a list of needed coinages. You can consider this a challenge, and if you'd like to test a new word of your own, be my guest.

ANTICIMPATIENCE is that near-your-goal urgency. That's long, but it's shorter than AREWETHEREYETNOFORTHEUMPTEENTHTIME.

* * *

An odd sound is an AUDITY.

* * *

Some of us prefer a climate with both warmth and COLDTH.

* * *

Highway construction often isn't construction. It may be just repair or maintenance. Let's have a word covering all such work with striped orange barrels and traffic cones: CRAM (Construction, Repair, And Maintenance) is descriptive, short for simpler signage, and describes the resulting traffic condition.

* * *

When a coined word doesn't have staying power, its fate is DISCOINAGE.

* * *

FANARCHY is riotous crowd behavior.

* * *

When you're both flustered and frustrated, you become FLUSTRATED.

* * *

When drizzle freezes on the highway, it becomes dangerous FRIZZLE.

* * *

True heroes, especially the gallant and valiant GALLIANTS, are rare.

* * *

A jogger who jiggles just has to be called a JOGGLER, doesn't she?

* * *

There sits the missile in its silo. It's remote, deep in the ground, and certainly not your farmer's silo. Let's call it a MISSILO.

* * *

NOTAB (None Of The ABove) is, like NIMBY (the dictionary-ensconced "Not In My Back Yard"), really an acronym, but surely qualifies for word status and maybe even a place on election ballots.

* * *

An unsightly junkyard in full view along the roadside is OBSCENERY.

* * *

Shouldn't an ORTHODONTIST be called an ORTHODENTIST?

* * *

PECANDY is for you if you like pecans and other good stuff mixed together.

* * *

PLIP-PLOP is the sleep-inducing sound of raindrops on tulip tree leaves.

* * *

A redundance that's dumb would be more descriptive as a redundance itself. Let's try REDUMBDUNCE.

* * *

When you ask someone if they'll do something for you, it's both a question and a request. A REQUESTION, if you please.

* * *

Son Rex points out that a sacrifice bunt attempt that fails should be called a SACRIFORCE. Still sacrificial, shouldn't we allow a merchant to call it a SACRIPRICE if he sells it below cost?

* * *

Isn't a sound bite on TV also a SIGHT BITE? (And don't you often want to bite back?)

* * *

The South must envy the North's many varieties of snow, such as granular SNOWFLECKS, unseasonal SNOWFLUKES, and zesty SNOWFLICKS along with the flaky stuff.

* * *

A summer calm is often TORN ATHUNDER by a thudden... er, sudden... storm.

* * *

VOLUNTYRRANY is punishment we self-inflict. TV, for example.

* * *

If something is very very yucky, it's VOMITABLE. It may even be bad enough to produce VOMIRRHEA.

* * *

A WEATHERSHED is the watershed date when the season's average temperature, precipitation, or other weather effect is at its highest or lowest.

* * *

A prostitute working despite job stress may earn a WHORES DE COMBAT citation.

* * *

You drive along the interstates and occasionally see a length of the old highway, maybe overgrown with weeds so that the pavement barely shows through. These are YESTERWAYS, sometimes maintained as access roads or private drives.

Coinages from other mint-ers

Joel Stein, in the June 21, 2010 issue of *Time*, gives us BUYCOTT as the opposite of boycott. We needed that one.

***

Sports report: "They turned the ball over twice after the CLEAN JERSEYS had taken over." Which tells you the subs finally got in the game.

***

George Will mentioned the "CNN-IZATION of our civilization." Probably based on CNN's news precocity and pervasiveness, well illustrated by Bernard Shaw's announcement from his CNN vantage point in Baghdad that the 1990-91 Gulf War had begun.

***

Oberlin College defines DORMCEST as dating or engaging in a sexual relationship with someone who lives in the same dormitory.

***

Today's DRIVE-BY POINT OF VIEW, a coinage by Mike Barnicle of the *Boston Globe*, has little patience with deliberation, and favors destruction of another's argument instead of debating it.

***

Jim Pawlak, Detroit columnist, said that EDGE-UCATION describes "cutting edge" skill-building seminars and special courses.

***

A GLIBERAL, says Paul Greenberg of the *Arkansas Democrat-Gazette*, is a glib liberal.

***

HE SAID, SHE SAID suggests a "who knows?" situation. The term was used often in reports of the Anita Hill-Clarence Thomas hearings in 1991.

* * *

William Safire's name for a dictionary of quotations is QUOTATIONARY.

* * *

Our local TV meteorologist said that a weather system had SCOOTCHED up from the South. That's more graphic than a simple "moved" up.

* * *

Another local pressperson reported that a woman scorned was a victim of SCORNMENT.

* * *

Still another local writer told of a person "... trying to SCRINCH the lid off." That's a good word because it describes both the facial contortions and the muscular effort needed to twist off the stubborn lid.

* * *

SINUENDO is a national pundit's term for Washingtonians' talk about capitol behavior.

* * *

Lewis Carroll's SLITHY (combining slimy and lithe) failed, regrettably, to earn dictionary acceptance.

* * *

Cities on the leeward side of large lakes, like Erie's Cleveland and Buffalo, have SNOWBURBS that are often victimized by especially heavy snowfalls, said a local coiner.

* * *

THINKUBATOR is the creative right side of the brain, suggests Detroit columnist Jim Pawlak.

* * *

WOOMPH is the sound a semi makes as it blows by, says an article in the *National Geographic*. It's a word with oomph.

Now it's your turn . . . the language-needy await your creativity and answers

Since professional wrestling isn't wrestling, it cries out for a descriptive word. "Staged mayhem" is a possibility, but I believe you can do better.

* * *

A newspaper story about ". . . Smith's 50-year-old boyfriend . . ." shows the need for a term (preferably a gender-neutral one) to identify a person beyond the girl/boy age with romantic linkage to another. "Companion" and "friend" aren't intimate enough, and "significant other" is too cumbersome.

* * *

At some point, your kids are no longer "children." Can't we come up with something better than "progeny" or "offspring" for these adults?

***

Do you suppose we'll ever have a good gender-neutral pronoun? "It" is too shaky. ("You had a phone call, but it didn't say its name.") "Guy(s)" is useful only as a plural, and is still a bit too slangy for general use. "He/she" is a wimpy copout. "Person" fits only sometimes. This could well be the toughest new-word challenge of all.

***

Where is the verb that describes the sex act with more delicacy than the four-letter one? "Sleep with" sidesteps the issue and is ambiguous. Send me your thoughts in a brown paper bag.

***

"Landlord" sounds medieval. Can't we give this person a contemporary title that's not so intimidating?

***

"Iowa advances caucuses to Jan. 24," said a headline. That's not clear. "Advance" probably means "earlier" in the context of the headline, but the word means to go forward, and in that sense Jan. 24 is a later date. "Delay" or "postpone" suffices for later. Now we need a verb for "set sooner."

***

If you must announce your intention to go to the bathroom, those are probably the words you use. But on the occasions when you need to be specific about it, what is the polite term? Must we settle for "number one" and "number two"? Or the children's wee-wee and doo-doo? On some occasions pee and poop will do. Should we just flush this question away?

* * *

The actor you like best is your favorite. But what do you call the one at the bottom of your list—your least favorite? Or your unfavorite? Surely there's a better word.

* * *

A biographer wrote of "the late Abigail Adams." Wouldn't "very late" have been more descriptive, since the lady expired a long time ago? And for someone who died just a few months ago, how about "the recent John Doe"?

* * *

You live on a picturesque acre, bordered on three sides by trees, with a lake to the west. Would you describe your property as being surrounded on three sides by trees? No, because "surrounded" means encircled and, like "pregnant," isn't subject to partlys or sort-ofs or gaps. Must we make do with "almost surrounded" or "semi-circled"?

* * *

"First come, first served" seems a cumbersome way to describe seating or service. "The early bird gets the worm" is also too long and wouldn't be appropriate for something like a spaghetti dinner. Don't just stand there, coin something!

WHAT A FIX WE'VE GOTTEN OURSELVES INTO!

Our unindisrespectednessly careless application of affixes—both prefixes and suffixes—has given us a usage mess that is probably beyond fixing. Consider:

Prefix has a prefix but suffix has no suffix—just a prefix—and it's really a postfix.

* * *

Sometimes you can't trust an adverb's prefix to stay true when it slips into noundom. For example, unjust becomes injustice. And that "in" can be negative as for inadequate, or positive as for invaluable.

* * *

Some "uns" can be dissed with no appreciable difference, as when unorganized becomes disorganized.

* * *

Habitable and inhabitable mean the same. To express "not inhabitable" only a double prefix will do: uninhabitable. Same with the flammable/inflammable/uninflammable trio.

* * *

Is a second capitulation a recapitulation? If yesterday's presentation was encored today, was it represented?

When the couch was covered again, was it recovered? Yes to all, but only if you sneak in a hyphen after each "re."

* * *

Distrust and mistrust mean pretty much the same thing, but displace and misplace don't. Distakes and mistortions like this are land mines in our word field.

* * *

Speaking of mises, you gotta be careful—even to the point of adding a hyphen in a word that doesn't need it. Example from a newspaper story: "Somehow the ball sliced like a mishit 3-iron . . ." As you see, if that three-letter prefix is treated as a two-letter syllable, as is the mi in migod, you could be in deep doo doo. Let's face it: mis is a mischievous miscreant. As a prefix to misled, it dignifies led, apparently not caring what that does to titled.

* * *

Is it -able as in laughable, or -ible as in divisible? Same problem with -ent/-ant (salient/deviant), -ence/-ance (adherence/deliverance), and -or/-er (creator/reporter). Sufferin' suffixes!

* * *

"Ex" can't make up its mind. It's pronounced eks in except, extra, experience, extreme, and lots of others. But it's eggs in exact, examine, and exert. Worse, it changes within the same family: An executive (eggs-ecutive) executes (eks-ecutes), and the exhibition (eks-ibition) contains many exhibits (eggs-ibits). Which proves that all your eggs won't fit in one basket, and all your ex's may live in Texas but eks's are widely scattered.

***

When an appointment is withdrawn, it is not a disappointment. Well, maybe sometimes. Notwithstanding means withstanding ... sort of. "Notwithstanding (despite) the order to stop, he proceeded ..." means that he disobeyed the order ... he withstood it. However, we're probably stuck with that "not" prefix unless we decide to abandon the word entirely and go with "despite" or "in spite of," which is not a bad idea.

WORD WEEDS

My research reveals several word weeds in our language field. For example, I found not one scene of Errol Flynn's movies ever showed the man buckling a swash, or even displaying one. I've also learned that tribulations always require trials, that flotsam and jetsam are seldom seen apart, that gall is never mitigated, and that you'll find what you lost much quicker if you look in both the crannies and the nooks.

* * *

Members of my scavenger hunt team couldn't find an old non-oaken bucket, or a non-distressed damsel, or an unoccupied tuffet. And, despite the fact that people are often left in them, not one lurch turned up.

* * *

I find it strange that only thirst is slaked, that newspapers never report timely deaths, that aspersions can be cast but never withdrawn, and that you can clench only your fist, teeth, and jaw.

* * *

At a baseball game the other day, I witnessed a brawl in the infield. But it was ruled illegal by the ump since it wasn't bench-clearing and they went at each other only with tongs, forgetting their hammers.

* * *

WORD WEEDS

A politician I know—formerly dissed but now sheveled and gruntled—ascribes his low dudgeon to the fact that his campaign remarks were blown into proportion just as he was being quoted in context. He didn't get the nomination, but was dumped ceremoniously. He felt that he was given long shrift, and he was able to adjust the fineness of both his fettle and his kettle of fish. He was like a man down the creek with a paddle—tickled red and acting like a sung hero.

* * *

A friend of mine has to see a cardiologist often because women keep playing around with his heart's cockles and strings, slowly wearing them away. He's now down to two or three of each.

* * *

A neighbor's feisty kid took the bull by the horn and went out for his high school's wrestling team, which he failed to make because he couldn't get his fell swoops down to one. In the process of losing his first practice match, he decided to forget the whole thing, but his shoulders were pinned and he couldn't find anything to shrug

* * *

More discoveries: brooks do nothing but babble, there is no clean lucre, and rotten things always wind up in Denmark. And I still haven't found out whether you can be on cloud nine and in seventh heaven at the same time.

* * *

I think I've discovered the secret of Seven Up's success: the inventor performed one-upmanship on six competitors.

* * *

Did you know that you can go half hog in some situations? You can, for example, get off with light punishment if you pull only one shenanigan, provided you have at least one or two scruples. And if you're only partly to blame, you can probably get by with making just one amend.

* * *

Newsflash: On the street yesterday I saw Willy without Nilly and Topsy without Turvy. The neighbors aren't yet very upset about it, being still down in arms.

* * *

Three sharks were arrested last week near Santa Cruz, California, and charged with disappointing tourists. Turns out that all three failed to infest the water, seemingly satisfied just to inhabit it.

* * *

By the way, you can believe every word of the above because I went off full-cocked.

* * *

Have a clement day.

AMERICAN ENGLISH ENLIVENS "DEAD"

Let's eavesdrop:

AT AN AIR-SEA RESCUE STATION: "I saw the island **dead** ahead—proof that my **dead** reckoning was **dead**-on. The sea was **dead** calm, but I had to make a **dead** stick landing. I figured I could be **dead** in the water . . . a **dead** duck."

* * *

AT A NIGHT CLUB: "It was a **dead** group. My act, normally a knock-'em **dead** shtick, was **dead** on arrival this night. I died on stage because I had a **dead** mike and the crowd seemed **dead** set against me, as lively as the walking **dead**. I got only **dead**pan looks and **dead** silence. I was at a **dead** end. I had a **dead**line to meet so I left, hoping I had time to commit two or three of the seven **dead**ly sins before the **dead** of night."

* * *

AT A BASKETBALL GAME: "This **dead**eye dude, always **dead** serious and never bothered by **dead** ball fouls, is a **dead** shot from any angle, even on a **dead** run. When he takes **dead** aim in a **dead** even game, you can be **dead** sure his defender is **dead** meat and the **dead**lock is history."

* * *

AMERICAN ENGLISH ENLIVENS "DEAD"

AT A POLICE STATION: "I thought the truck driver was **dead** to the world, but he was **dead** as a doornail, with a bullet hole **dead** center in the back of his head. He had just returned from a **dead**head run and must've been **dead** drunk because he had trouble jimmying the **dead**bolt. He seemed to be a **dead** ringer for the guy we wanted **dead** or alive. Anyway, we had him **dead** to rights and it was a **dead** issue. I tried to lift him, but I was **dead** tired and he was a **dead**weight."

* * *

AT A PARKING LOT: "It seemed a **dead** cinch that the drop-**dead** gorgeous blonde sitting **dead** still in the car was playing **dead,** probably to scare a **dead**beat husband. It was the **dead** of winter, so probably a **dead** battery kept the car **dead** in its tracks. Such **dead**head stunts are **dead** giveaways."

* * *

AT THE RACETRACK: "The win and place horses finished in a **dead** heat, but the show horse died in the stretch and faded to **dead** last. The jockey didn't whip him because he saw no point in beating a **dead** horse. Some people may have thought he was **dead** wrong, but I thought he was **dead** right."

Multiple-use words abound. You can charge ahead, charge a battery, charge a purchase, charge a suspect with a crime, or charge a person with responsibility. And you'll get a real charge out of five other common words: set, break, turn, take, and run. They have, respectively, 119, 122, 122, 124, and 179 definitions in my big, fat unabridged dictionary.

HELP!

Hey folks, I need your help. Several things have been bothering me since Hector was a pup, and if you're as old as I am you know that's been a long time. If you can answer any of the following questions for me, I'll be obliged.

When did "heading south" become a negative? ("He lost his job, his car, and his wife—his whole life was heading south.") And why don't Southerners object to the term? Is it because all maps put the South down and they've just learned to live with it?

* * *

"Like father, like son" is an expression that makes little sense when you pick at it. Who is this person who's like both of them?

* * *

Before furniture was upholstered, was it first holstered—maybe somewhere out West? By a cowboy?

* * *

Are powwow and bowwow our only 3-w words? Is knickknack our only word with four k's? Are Keokuk, Kankakee, and Kaskaskia our only 3-k towns? Are screeched, stretched, strengths, and scrounged our longest one-syllable words? These are worrisome questions!

* * *

HELP!

"Fridge" is a shortening of refrigerator, which has no d. "No." is the abbreviation for number, which has no o. When the pope becomes papal, he replaces his o and e with two a's but we don't call him papa as the Italians do. Why... why... why?

* * *

Entrée is French for entry. So if we take the French at their word shouldn't the appetizer be called an entrée, with a different name for the main course?

* * *

Will someone tell me when and why "hanging in the fire" was compressed into "hanging fire"? And why hasn't "changing the sheets" become "changing sheets"?

* * *

I must have been about twelve when I figured out that "he nodded" meant yes, and "he shook his head" meant no. Really now, couldn't either term fit either action?

* * *

Is anything spindly but legs? Are most fits of the conniption type?

* * *

The word "can" has its "can't, so why doesn't "will" have its "willn't"? And when your will power enables you to stop smoking, shouldn't it be called won't power?

* * *

Among the pronouns (I, you, me, us, they, she, it, etc.), only I is capitalized. Why?

* * *

Conservatives and conservationists often aren't on the same side, but shouldn't they be?

* * *

And why does "feminist" tend to harden "feminine"?

* * *

There's an Old South and an Old West but the East and the North don't get such romantic attention. Is geographic discrimination at work here?

* * *

Shouldn't a specimen be a speciman when it comes from one man? It's an even bigger question when the specimen is from a woman.

* * *

Who is responsible for injecting "ta" where it doesn't belong? It just adds a needless syllable to preventative, authoritative, and commentator, among others. Combative looks fine without one. So does adaptive. And can you imagine creative as creatative? I move that we say ta ta to ta. Do I hear a second?

* * *

Shouldn't molten steel be called melten steel?

* * *

Do you get momentarily confused by the same-starting but opposite-meaning words secular and sectarian? I invariably do. I blame it on their bi-secs-ism.

When an indictment is quashed isn't it also squashed? Why do we need quash?

* * *

"We ain't never seen nobody..." is a triple negative from a newspaper story. If a double negative creates a positive, does a triple one restore the negative? Would a quadruple one ("I can't give nothin' to nobody never") bring back the positive? Isn't this a great language?

* * *

Why do you pay a compliment but level a criticism?

* * *

A newspaper story said "There's a growing awareness of how fun and easy it is." When did "how fun" replace "how much fun?" Just askin'. And "more fun" often becomes "funner." You wouldn't say "how enjoyment," but you could say "how enjoyable" and "more enjoyable," a luxury that fun doesn't have. "Funner" and "funnest" aren't yet respectable, but the sheer weight of usage will probably change that before long. It's overdue.

BREAKING YOUR WORD

Bad breaks at a line's end can turn a therapist into the-rapist, and manslaughter into mans-laughter . . . almost reversing the meanings.

* * *

That pesky hyphen can screw things up even in the middle of a line. A local newspaper story said that a popular TV personality had resigned, when in fact she had re-signed. A printed clarification the next day restored the AWOL hyphen, reassuring her fans that she had signed on again.

* * *

I collect coins. My favorites are the ones created by the hyphen at line breaks: coin-surance, coin-cidence, and coin-ventor.

* * *

The Hebrides Islands became oxymoronic when a misguided syllable-separator came up with He-brides. And the father of medicine had to add "packager of large animals" to his resume when Hippocrates became Hippo-crates.

* * *

Because it's important to nail a child molester, let's don't mis-identify him as a mole by breaking him into a mole-ster. Same with mole-sting (moles don't sting, in any case). And, if you're not careful, molestation could

BREAKING YOUR WORD

be that yard bump where the mole stations itself to rest and dine.

∗ ∗ ∗

Was her tight dress adjustment a re-arrangement or a rear-rangement? And when the fugitive was re-arrested he probably wasn't rear-rested.

∗ ∗ ∗

Do men swear? Of course. But the ad meant to say "men's wear." Was the TV station talking about its news team or its new steam?

∗ ∗ ∗

The caption "Incapable hands" for the publicity picture of the company's new president would have upset a lot of people if the proofreader hadn't made a pre-print fix: "In capable hands."

Line breaks can also result in embarrassment, like this newspaper headline whose problem is even more glaring when the two lines are separated by the fold of the paper:

FINANCE HEAD EMILY COX GETS LAID
---------------------(fold)--------------------------
OFF DUE TO CITY STAFF DOWNSIZING

The headline writer could have kept Emily from storming into the newsroom if he'd managed to keep "laid off" on the same line.

54

OPPOSITES

(Words or expressions with opposite or near-opposite meanings)

ALL OVER. It means everywhere, also gone, finished.

* * *

A PART . . . APART. She was a part of his life before they drifted apart.

* * *

AWFUL. It used to mean full of awe, but it has migrated to terrible.

* * *

BACKUP. On your flight to Mars you'll want a backup system for waste disposal in case there's a backup in the primary system. (What a relief for relievers!)

* * *

BENCH. A judge on the bench is part of the courtroom action. A football player on the bench is out of the action. And the Cincinnati Reds' Johnny Bench was anything but a bench player.

* * *

BETRAY. If you betray (reveal) affection for her, you're in her favor. But if you betray (violate) her trust, you're out the door.

* * *

BIG BROTHER. He can be a sinister observer ("Big Brother is watching"), or a mentor for a fatherless child.

* * *

BOLT. You bolt a door to secure it, or bolt through it to escape.

* * *

BOMB. A long forward pass for a touchdown is a bomb. So is a stage play that flops.

* * *

BREAK. A break in the weather gave you clear sailing for your trip, but a break in your car's electrical connection kept you from going. Those are the breaks.

* * *

BUCKLE. You buckle your seat belt for safety. But your knees might buckle under a too-heavy load.

* * *

BUST. The general's bust immortalized him, but the corporal who wrote "for the pigeons" on it was busted to private.

* * *

CITATION. You may be cited for bravery, or for doing 50 in a 30 zone.

* * *

CLEAVE. It means both "to adhere to" and "to split apart." So Cleaveland became Cleveland to avoid such confusion? Not really. A long-ago writer omitted the first a of founder Moses Cleaveland's last name and the error lingered in the city's name. This may have been the very first "mistake on the lake."

* * *

CLIP. After you clip a piece of paper into pieces with your scissors, you can put 'em together with a paper clip.

* * *

COP. The beat cop is the good guy. The shoplifter who cops stuff is a bad guy.

* * *

CRITICIZE. A critic's comments can be complimentary or helpful. Or a kick in the pants.

* * *

CROWN. She was crowned prom queen, but she was so boastful that the runner-up could have crowned her.

* * *

CUT. Joe's cut was $50, but Sam was cut out of the pot.

* * *

DIRT. Grimy stuff for the dustpan, but growing stuff for the garden.

* * *

DOWNHILL. "It's all downhill from here" can be great if it means you can now relax and soon enjoy the fruits of a job well done, but it could also mean you've done your best and face bleak prospects.

* * *

DRESS. She looks great when she dresses up, but if something is out of place she'll get a dressing-down from her fashion designer.

* * *

DROP. When Al dropped his plan to drop in on Amy, he may have ended a promising relationship.

* * *

DUST. Crop dusters apply it, furniture dusters remove it.

* * *

ENGAGEMENT. A romantic tie, and a military battle. Some would see a parallel.

* * *

EXECUTE. To accomplish. Or to kill.

* * *

FIGHT WITH. Al fights with (beside) Jim to defeat Roy and Tom. Then Al and Jim fight with (against) each other to determine top dog.

* * *

FILE. A reporter files a story with his editor for tomorrow's edition, but the story may get killed by filing it away.

* * *

FINALLY. In his final (last time) try for the top, he finally (first time) reached it.

* * *

FIRE. A house on fire can kill people inside the building. And an "on-fire" stage performer can "kill the people" in a sold-out house.

* * *

FIX. A fixed fight is quite different from a fixed lawnmower. And "I'll fix your clock" is great if said by your clock repairman, but somewhat ominous if it comes from an angry neighbor.

* * *

FLAG. Positively patriotic as a noun, but generally negative as a verb.

* * *

FORGE. You're a winner when you forge family unity and metal shapes, but you should stop before you get to checks and documents.

* * *

FOUNDER. One who founders in deep water is in trouble. But a founder of an enterprise may get rich.

* * *

GROUNDED. Do your homework and you'll become well-grounded in your school subjects. Neglect it and you could be grounded . . . car-less and Carla-less for a week.

* * *

HANDICAP. It's a plus in contested events because it brings you up to your competitors' level. But a physical handicap usually produces a disadvantage.

* * *

HELLUVA. He may be a helluva manager, but his neglect of his wife is a helluva way to treat a lady.

* * *

HUSTLE. Pete Rose hustled on the field and won. He hustled bets and lost.

* * *

INCREDIBLE. A hawker's "incredible" offer is often not credible.

* * *

KICKOFF. Starts a football game, ends a life.

* * *

KILL. (See FIRE.)

* * *

KNOCKOUT. A ten-count for a boxing loser, a ten for the beauty contest winner.

* * *

LOVE. It makes the world go 'round, but it's nothing to a tennis player.

* * *

OUT. It means emergence when "the word is out," but disappearance when a word is no longer fashionable. And

OPPOSITES

when the stars and secrets are out they're on display, but when the lights and the fires are out they're gone.

* * *

OVERLOOK. If you forgot to stop at the scenic view, you overlooked the overlook.

* * *

OVERSIGHT. When the committee on oversight goofed, it committed an oversight.

* * *

PARBOIL. It means both to boil fully and for just a short time. The word confuses recipe readers.

* * *

PILL. Prescribed pills help keep you well, but that ornery kid is a hard-to-take pill.

* * *

PITS. A pitted road surface has pits. Pitted olives don't.

* * *

PRETTY. Things have come to a pretty pass (are you old enough to remember this bad-situation idiom?) if all you need to get a job is a pretty face.

* * *

PROFILING. An essential tool for law enforcement, but prejudicial if improperly used.

* * *

PROTEST. It's an objection. It's also an affirmation.

PUT OUT. The tenants were put out by the fire that the firemen put out.

* * *

RAVE. "To utter in madness or frenzy" or to praise highly.

* * *

RECALL. When the voters recall an elected official, he's out of a job. When a teacher is recalled, she gets her job back.

* * *

RENTED ROOM. It pays landlords, costs tenants.

* * *

SANCTION. Sanctions (coercions) against Iraq were sanctioned (approved) by the U.N.

* * *

SCAN. Let's go right to the dictionary. One definition: "To investigate thoroughly by checking point by point." Another: "To glance from point to point, often hastily, casually."

* * *

SEED. Seeding puts seeds in a garden, removes them from cherries.

* * *

SIGHT. You're a sight for sore eyes, but your messy room is a sight.

* * *

SIGN OFF. The mayor signed off on the document (started an action) before she signed off at five p.m. (ended the workday).

* * *

SMITTEN. New Orleans was smitten by lethal Katrina. John was smitten by lovely Kate.

* * *

STRIKE. When the parties strike a deal, they confirm an agreement. But union workers confirm a disagreement when they strike.

* * *

STRIKE OUT. Bad for batters, good for bowlers.

* * *

SUBMIT. This come-and-go word lets you proffer or yield.

* * *

TEMPER. Tempering hardens steel but softens a penalty by tempering justice with mercy.

* * *

THROW IN. If you throw in with a group, you join it. But when you throw in your cards or throw in the towel, you're backing out.

* * *

TOAST. He's toast if he loses soundly, but his toast is tasty with coffee.

* * *

TOWBOAT. Those Mississippi towboats behind the barges are pushers. So, basically, are those tugboats in harbors, nudging big ships into position for docking. I haven't seen much towing by towboats or tugging by tugboats.

* * *

TRAILER. It previews a movie, but follows a vehicle.

* * *

TRIM. You trim the Christmas tree first by removing growth to shape it, then by adding decorations for adornment.

* * *

UNQUALIFIED. As support it's the best, but it's the worst label for a job applicant.

* * *

WAKE. It's a watch at the funeral home before burial, or a prelude to rising in the morning.

* * *

WASHED UP. Your persistent failure to wash up for dinner could wash up your reputation for cleanliness.

* * *

WEIGH. If the captain forgets to weigh (bring up) the anchor, it may weigh on his mind.

* * *

WIND UP. A wind up starts a pitch or a clock, but finishes a job or a speech.

Same meaning for opposite words

When the alarm goes OFF it goes ON.

* * *

Both FAT CHANCE and SLIM CHANCE give you almost no chance.

* * *

If you're charged with being LEGALLY DRUNK, it would be a mistake to deny it by claiming instead that you were ILLEGALLY DRUNK.

* * *

Both SHARP TALK and BLUNT TALK can be cutting.

* * *

He GAVE IN (and UP) when his stamina gave OUT.

* * *

Ira got a GOOD LICKING. Lou got a BAD LICKING. Both were well-licked.

* * *

There's not much difference between BUILD ON and BUILD OFF OF.

* * *

UP and DOWN often have identical meanings. A car breaks DOWN or UP, a marriage breaks UP or DOWN. The building that burns UP also burns DOWN. Whether a job winds UP or winds DOWN, it's completed. When a barber shuts his door for the day, he closes UP . . . and DOWN. A rain is heavy when it keeps UP coming DOWN.

***

The ASCENT OF MAN and the DESCENT OF MAN are both journeys through time in the same direction.

***

It's easier for an entertainer to become HOT if he's COOL.

You don't say!

Do you HOPE AGAINST HOPE that they'll find the lost kid? Not really. You want your hopes to be *for* discovery, not against. You don't want one hope canceling another.

***

"She saved money AGAINST THE DAY when Joey started college." But she meant *for* the day.

***

COULDN'T CARE LESS is almost always the meaning intended by those who say they could care less.

***

FUHGEDABOUDIT, a relatively recent coinage with many spellings, means remember it. It's a sports announcer's term that heralds a homerun with enough distance or drama to make it memorable.

***

YOU DON'T SAY! is an acknowledgement of what you did say.

***

When you're told that YOU WON'T BELIEVE THIS, you're supposed to believe it.

* * *

NO MEAN TASK describes a mean task.

* * *

TO COIN A PHRASE introduces a well-known (not coined) phrase.

* * *

People who say I HATE TO SAY I TOLD YOU SO love to say they told you so.

* * *

I DON'T MEAN TO PRY is an assurance by someone about to pry.

* * *

NOT TO CHANGE THE SUBJECT precedes a change in subject.

* * *

When you say of a bad person, I HOPE HE CAN SLEEP AT NIGHT, what you really mean is you hope he can't. You probably even hope he's miserable.

* * *

YEAH, SURE means approximately "no way."

* * *

The candidate who STANDS for office RUNS for it.

* * *

HEAD OVER HEELS means heels over head.

* * *

YOUR POINT IS WELL-TAKEN means your point is well given.

* * *

RECORDS ARE MEANT TO BE BROKEN is not only a ridiculous statement, it is somewhat of an insult to the record-holder. Swimmer Mark Spitz didn't set seven world records in the 1972 Munich Olympics in order to surrender his place in the Guinness book to Michael Phelps' "Eight in '08" performance in Beijing. The longer a record lasts, the more its holder can be (and no doubt is) proud of it. If the statement read "Records are inevitably broken," it would make more sense.

* * *

TELL ME ABOUT IT means don't tell me about it. I already know. It's old stuff.

* * *

A SPEED BUMP is actually a slow-down bump.

* * *

DOWN EAST is up if you live south of Maine. Most of us do.

Chaff in the field of opposites

RAZE and RAISE are same-sound words with opposite meanings. So are HEROIN and HEROINE. And these come close: VIRAL and VIRILE.

* * *

RADIATION and IRRADIATION are similar. So are BONE and DEBONE, BONED and BONELESS, RAVEL and UNRAVEL, FOUL and BEFOUL, BAR and DEBAR.

* * *

If you remember when an IRONER was called a MANGLE, did you ever wonder about the contradiction in terms?

* * *

A politician complained of an UNTRUE MISCONCEPTION, forgetting that a double negative creates a positive.

* * *

A story that's full of holes is made up OUT OF WHOLE CLOTH.

* * *

The critic was held in RAPT attention by the play he RAPPED.

* * *

When you think about what that dog has been licking and eating, you probably won't use the phrase CLEAN AS A HOUND'S TOOTH again.

* * *

THEATER OF WAR seems a contradiction in terms unless carnage is entertainment, as when the gladiators became lion fare.

* * *

SPEND and THRIFT just don't make sense as one word.

* * *

He TURNED UP MISSING raises the question: where did he turn up?

* * *

When the sportswriter told us that the football team "struggled to get their offense UNTRACKED," he meant "on track." It's a common error, mostly by sports reporters. I don't know why.

* * *

SCIENCE and SEANCE sound pretty much alike, but the meanings are as different as truth and fiction.

* * *

In baseball, a CHANGEUP is a pitched ball that's slower than the batter expects. In other words, it's a CHANGE DOWN in speed. Speaking of ups and downs, I punched the wrong button in an elevator and ended up down.

MAN HANDLING

Upright, respectable words are dying. Some are just withering for lack of use. Many are being shot down by political correctors.

"Schoolmarm" bit the dust about the time Gary Cooper gunned down the black hats around high noon. Except in the South, "ma'am" is on life support. "Freshman" is now threatened by "first year student" and "freshperson."

* * *

Columnist Ellen Goodman used the word "gentlepersonly," apparently abhorring "gentlemanly."

* * *

A New York woman named Donna Ellen Cooperman went to court to have her name changed to Donna Ellen Cooperperson. Newspaper report, April 13, 1995. Honest.

* * *

We must stop this bleeding. I hereby propose a "protected words" program to defend Manhattan, Manitoba, Manila, Mandalay, and The Isle of Man. And let us...

(1) hold inviolate manuscript, manufacture, manslaughter, manual, manmade, straw man, middleman, manhandle, statesmanship, oneupmanship, and that icon built lovingly every year by millions of kids: the snowman, and...

(2) allow Man-O-War to rest undisturbed in horse heaven, and . . .

(3) sanctify "One small step for a man, one giant leap for mankind," "Greater love hath no man," "The best laid plans of mice and men," "Simple Simon met a pieman," "Time and tide wait for no man," "No man is an island," "Man's inhumanity to man," "A dog is man's best friend," "All men are created equal," and . . .

(4) perhaps most difficult of all for female-type persons, let us put up with the men in menstruate, menopause, hymen, specimen, and (take a deep breath now) women.

Guys, unless we can reverse the tide, we may have to person the lifeboats.

PLURALSY

Pluralsy is one of the afflictions of our language. The things that can happen to an innocent noun when it goes from single status to plural seem endless. For example:

We're awash in plural forms: chair/chairs, watch/watches, self/selves, sty/sties, mouse/mice, ox/oxen, datum/data, criterion/criteria, radius/radii.

* * *

A berry becomes berries, but Jim Berry and his family are comfortable as the Berrys.

* * *

"Axes" is the plural of both axe and axis. You need context to ascertain meaning.

* * *

Some nouns look singular but can also be plural: fish, deer, elk, aircraft. And, although goose goes to geese, moose stays moose. Functioning singular but looking plural are annals, alms, forceps, lens, scissors, trousers. And you won't see a boondock, smithereen, sud, or oop alone. Or a husting. Let's face it, navigating through this mess requires more than a GPS.

* * *

Nouns ending in "f" take different paths to their plurals. Dwarf, scarf, and wharf allow you to add "s" or to change the "f" to "ves." But for half, wolf (usually), elf, self, shelf, and loaf you have only the "ves" option. Spoof, proof, roof, and reef keep the simple "s." Enough with the –f words already.

* * *

That famous "word from our sponsor" may well be a hundred words or more. A singular exaggeration.

* * *

This from George Carlin, author of *Braindroppings*, a very funny book: What's the plural of "helluva guy" as in "He's a helluva guy"? The nominations are open.

* * *

If "a yardful of weeds" is the way to say it, why not "a headful of hairs"?

* * *

We say that a chimp runs on "all fours," but since we're talking about just one set of four limbs, and even though no chimp has ever complained about the expression, it seems to me that we should say "all four."

SNICKERS

Antipasto? No way. How can you be anti anything Italian?

* * *

Remember, if you bond with someone it's called bonding, not bondage.

* * *

The plural of Doberman is Dobermans, not Dobermen. And the female is still a Doberman, proving that—at least in dogdom—a "man" can be a bitch.

* * *

I feel sorry for the brethren. They have no sistren, fathren, or mothren.

* * *

Hey guys, before you propose, consider wedlock's second syllable.

* * *

You can be pretty sure that the praying mantis' prey doesn't have a prayer.

* * *

He's a chip off the old block and, like father like son, may follow in his father's footsteps. Boys will be boys so he'll have to be allowed to sow his wild oats. But he's never called fast, or an easy lay, or a tramp or slut. Fodder for feminists?

* * *

And then there's the English teacher who reads nothing but whodidits.

* * *

If an icebreaker breaks ice, does a windbreaker break wind?

* * *

Lust is an anagram of slut. Okay, who's responsible for this?

* * *

A newspaper story reported that "The second Million-Youth March drew about 2,000 people (police estimated less than 1,000) to the streets of Harlem yesterday." The rally also drew about 1,500 policemen—what you might call a million-man police presence.

* * *

The "four corners of the world" coiner likely failed both geometry and geography.

* * *

Maybe excrement should be the opposite of increment, but let's not push it.

* * *

Don't ride with anyone who answers "right" when you ask, "Should I make a left here?"

* * *

Son Rex says that our language itself reinforces the notion that women are expensive. "It's no accident that fiancée and finance are almost the same word."

* * *

She asked if I wanted help moving the furniture. I said no, I could do it singlehandedly. I was wrong. Turns out I needed both hands.

* * *

MOM is a WOW when she's upside down, but it's not very ladylike.

* * *

One who undertakes a project is not necessarily an undertaker.

* * *

Joe kept bugging Stan with word questions. "Is there a word with three u's?" and "Is abstemious the only English word with all five vowels in order?" and "Are sugar and sumac the only English words that begin with su pronounced shu?" Stan's answers were "If so, it's gotta be unusual" to the first question, "The facetious answer is "Yes" to the second one, and "Sure" to the third. Joe decided to take his questions elsewhere.

* * *

"Going to" has gone and "have to" has had it and we're just gonna hafta accept both.

* * *

"Dreampt" is abrupt and unkempt. Every time I hear it I get steampt. Forty lashes to dreampt. Forty winks to dreamed.

* * *

"Asteroid" is not a vulgarism for hemorrhoid. (And yes, I did have to look up hemorrhoid to be sure of its spelling).

* * *

The world's most carefully pronounced flower: fuchsia. The world's most carefully pronounced religious sect: Shi-ite. The world's most carefully pronounced dog: Shih Tzu. The world's most carefully pronounced baseball player: Kosuke Fukudome of the Chicago Cubs.

* * *

Bedridden is a strange word. The last thing you want to do when you're confined to bed is to ride or be ridden. (I said *confined* to bed.)

* * *

Guy buys a snake. Names it Alice. Spells it Alysssss, of course.

* * *

"He was buried in his work." Because he accepted interment after medical school?

* * *

We were talking about words with silent letters, like the b in plumbing and the p in psalm. Friend Merritt pointed out that another silent p—one rarely mentioned—is the one in swimming. He also volunteered that a fastidious person is often slowtidious.

*\ *\ *

Clinton's lawyers were "aggressively listening" to proposals. Those people really had a way with words.

*\ *\ *

A one-night stand isn't a stand, it's a lay. A lay preacher works standing. Standing water just lays there. It's time we stood for truth and stopped lying about our lays.

*\ *\ *

Weather forecasters need only a bunch of four-letter words to talk to us: rain, warm, snow, hazy, hail, gale, damp, heat, smog, mild, cold, fair, wind, mist, dank, dewy, calm seas, high surf, neap tide. Cool.

*\ *\ *

William Espy, in his *Game of Words*, says that the ten most frequent words in English are: the, of, and, to, a, in, that, it, is, and I. But that was before we were besieged by y'know, like, and whatever.

*\ *\ *

A word to the wise golfers: If you tell your wife you're going to play a round, be sure to add "of golf."

*\ *\ *

Spoonerisms are fun: shake a tower and take a shower, bad money and mad bunny, kid sister and Sid kissed her, A Tale of Two Cities and a sale of . . . well, you know.

*\ *\ *

I've heard that there is no English word with the precise meaning of the Jewish word chutzpah. I think it takes a lot of gall, nerve, balls, audacity, temerity, cheek, spunk, effrontery, presumption, moxie, and brazenness to say that.

* * *

Today's slanguage can be mercifully brief. The two syllables of "noam sain" require only 25% of the vocal time of "do you know what I am saying?"

* * *

TV panelist: "I would hope that we would move toward complete reporting." He's lost in the woulds. He needs a clearing.

* * *

Informal survey: 70% of our two-syllable words accent the first syllable, as do 21 of our 22 two-syllable presidents, all four two-syllable planets (gotta have Pluto for this one), four of our five two-syllable states, and 17 of our 20 largest two-syllable cities. Friend Jan from Erie wonders if I'm ever going to do anything productive with my time.

* * *

Claudia and I had some fun with the "you" and "oo" sounds of the letter u. She says puma is "poo-ma" and I say "pyoo-ma." Which led us to pupil's "pyoop-il" vs. "poop-il," and to puppy/pyuppy vs. poopy/pyoopy. Face it, folks: we don't have to look far for fun. Everyday words are full of it.

* * *

NE for Nebraska, OK for Oklahoma, DE for Delaware. Two capital letters, no periods. Great idea. Gets the mail through faster. Problem is, the Ohio city of North Olmsted copied the idea in its sign announcing the annual "NO Christmas Tree Lighting Ceremony." The people who called city hall weren't jolly.

* * *

The -teous in righteous is pronounced "chuss," but in beauteous it's "tee-us." Could be worse. We don't have to put up with wrongeous or uglyeous.

* * *

" -que" is queer. It produces a blike in oblique, a kay in risque, and an abrupt k in bisque . . . which makes each unique . . . er, you-neek. It's a cue in queue, a kwee or kay in Quebec, and has a "kw--" sound in queen and query. Banquet's ending is a quet, but parquet's is a kay. You can make a quiche quickly, but not a kweesh kickly.

* * *

The First Unitarian Church of Kennebunkport, Maine will attest to the fact that acronyms and abbreviations are sometimes just not appropriate.

* * *

Shouldn't "lisp" be pronounced "lithp"?

* * *

Pennsylvania's road signs say the state is "Fine for Littering." Georgia goes further, promising "$1000 for littering." But after easing off the pedal to a dangerously slow 65 to read the next such sign's fine print, I could make out the "up to" and "fine" flanking "$1000." My crest fell, ending my visions of enrichment-by-wastebasket-emptying.

* * *

On the road across Florida's Everglades, a sign—"Watch for panthers"—was followed shortly by another one—"Picnic table ahead." Unwilling to volunteer as a potential entrée, we moved right along.

* * *

We all talk too much. Always have. At about 15 months we learn that two words are better than one. We start with ma ma, da da, yum yum, wee wee, din din, no no, and boo boo. Then we're tipped off to goody goody, picky picky, hubba hubba (remember?), rah rah and hip hip hooray, tut tut, chop chop, and so on. By the time we get to doo doo we're in deep.

WATCH OUT FOR LOOSE BROADS

Make that "boards." You and I sometimes misread a word because it's much like another one with a different meaning. (Was that really a "calvary" charge?) In the sentences below, one of the words in each pair may be momentarily mistaken for the other because they're anagrams with the same first letter. But the differences in meaning are great, even though both words make sense in the sentence.

- To get the part, she would SIGN/SING anything.

- Many unwanted pregnancies are blamed on CAUSAL/CASUAL sex.

- He was resigned to death and TAXES/TEXAS, preferably in that order.

- Every Thanksgiving he CARVED/CRAVED the turkey.

- The MARITAL/MARTIAL arts belong in wedding plans.

- Is it wise to keep the home FIRES/FRIES burning?

- Some couples enjoy life more after they're UNITED/UNTIED.

- The play's producer succeeded because he worked the ANGLES/ANGELS.

WATCH OUT FOR LOOSE BROADS

- At the food center, there was BARLEY/BARELY enough to go around.

- The BULGE/BUGLE in his coat stopped him at the checkpoint.

- It was a GUTSY/GUSTY day as the home team won.

- Before leaving, they danced a MINUTE/MINUET.

- She didn't like his PROFILE/PROLIFE position.

- Sometimes it's smart to RESERVE/REVERSE your opinion.

- The canyon's great size produced a SCARED/SACRED feeling.

- The quarry was TRIED/TIRED.

- Some people dread the arrival of SANTA/SATAN.

- The band had several WEIRD/WIRED members.

- The tax auditor was a frequent FLIER/FILER.

And here's a "three-fer":

- A good start in life comes from PRENATAL/PARENTAL/PATERNAL care.

SOUND TRAPS

If people don't understand you, maybe it's your fault. Careless enunciation can be a problem. It's smart to be aware of the pitfalls, the sound traps. Like these:

A TV commercial for a garlic product featured a man and woman jogging together, accompanied by a voice-over assuring us that "we take gar-leek every day." I heard it as "we take our leek every day," probably because the k and hard g sounds are pretty much the same, and the ensuing "gar" is almost "our." Momentarily shocked, I did a double-take. But they were still jogging.

* * *

You're invited to a party. You don't like large gatherings, so you ask how many people are expected. "Four to six," is what you hear. So you go, and encounter forty-six persons. Mis-spoken or mis-heard?

* * *

The network newscaster told of "four to five hundred" Americans in Iraq ... or was it forty-five hundred? It matters.

* * *

"The biggest threat the president could encounter" might have been "... couldn't counter." Sometimes you wish for instant replay of broadcast news reports, so you'll know

SOUND TRAPS

whether the president said "we will not accept inaction," or was it "an action"? Big difference.

* * *

"Four teen girls died in the crash," said the newscaster. Migod, did she say fourteen?

* * *

Once in a while two different meanings can both be true, as in the report that Minneapolis residents were either isolated or ice elated following a winter storm.

* * *

Did I hear "all factory incentives" or "olfactory incentives"? Was it "Novak seen" or "no vaccine"? And, especially if you live in southwestern Ohio, "antioxidant" can sound like "Antioch sedan."

* * *

"UN approves a tax on pirates," said a friend, reading aloud from the newspaper about the UN's approval of "attacks." I vote for both.

* * *

If your mother lives near Toledo's river, you could call her your Maumee mommy. (I said it and I'm glad, even if I am the 8,229th person to do so.)

* * *

Surely Charles Schwab wasn't admitting to "forgetful commission brokers." No, he just wanted me to "forget full commission brokers."

* * *

"You and I" or "You and Di"? "Gemini" or "Jim and I"?

* * *

Do our hard-won rights depend on how hard one writes?

* * *

The ad suggestion to "drink Ensure® as a meal" can be heard as a weird claim that "drink insures a meal."

* * *

Claudia was reading a novel and came across this exchange:

"What's wrong with the baby?"
"He's got sickle cell anemia."
"Oh, my goddaughter's baby got sick as hell anemia too!"

* * *

"Did you say you heard a victim moan?" "No, I said I heard Vic Damone."

* * *

Moe Vaughan, the baseball player, probably often hears someone tell him to move on.

It's even worse when the meanings are opposite

"Can't tell" almost always sounds like "Can tell" because of those two close t's. Solution: "cannot" instead of "can't" and an emphasis on "can" in "can tell."

SOUND TRAPS

* * *

Two Olympic hockey teams met in a "winner go home" game. Or maybe it was "win or go home," which sends the loser home, which is surely the intended meaning.

* * *

More opposites from my broadcast file: Illegal alien/a legal alien, illegal dumping/a legal dumping, illegitimate reform/a legitimate reform, unnecessary/a necessary, it's now true/it's not true, inept person/an apt person, the risks of inaction/the risks of an action, a bright and crowded room/a bright uncrowded room, invisible/and visible.

* * *

It took a while for me to figure out that the radio commercial's "committed inactive" candidate was actually committed and active. But that wasn't as bad as the judicial candidate's commercial which told me that she "represented and offended" thousands of working people, probably losing some votes because she hadn't clearly "represented and defended" those people.

* * *

On "Larry King Live" he understood Janet Reno's "specific and credible" as "specific incredible." So did I. She had to renounce her enunciation.

* * *

From a crime scene report: "... the other and distinct shoeprint" is night-and-day different from "... the other indistinct shoeprint."

* * *

Your marriage could be saved or ruined, depending on whether she hears you say, "I'll believe in you" or "I'll be leavin' you."

On the blue side

If she says "I want my glove" but you hear "I wanta make love" and respond as any red-blooded man would, you could be an arrested (not a rested) person.

* * *

At the store I found that their ad was for a sectional sofa, not a sexual sofa.

* * *

Surely I'm not alone in hearing "Londonderry Air" as "London derriere."

* * *

TV promo for a basketball game: "Cavs in heat at the Coliseum tonight." But the fans were no doubt looking forward to the game between the Cleveland Cavaliers and the Miami Heat.

* * *

You take a call at the office for an absent co-worker and leave him a call-back number for "Dixie Moore." Excited, and perhaps hoping for a new romantic partner, your friend calls this woman whose name he doesn't recognize, but connects with the guy who found his wallet: Dick Seymour.

The recovery of his wallet's contents almost made up for his disappointment.

From my grab bag

Assemble/a symbol, black guys/black eyes, Uranus/your anus, climate/climb it, condom nation/condemnation, floor debate/Florida bait, game ends/gay men's, Grade A/gray day, home addition/home edition, if you expect it/a few expected, this scrap/this crap, that's tough/that stuff, your analysis/urinalysis, isle of view/I love you.

* * *

One more—it's a triple play, and it's my favorite: If you set your boat on cruise control you avoid the need for crew's control and the crews can troll.

HEY WEBSTER...

Yes, you—the guy with the dictionary. We need to talk.

It's time you had your COMEDOWNANCE. You call it comeuppance, which is surely a blatant example of misdirection. It's time you were cited for your sloppy performance.

* * *

Speaking of downs, if a guy gets an upbraiding he probably feels pretty down, so shouldn't he be the victim of a DOWNBRAIDING?

* * *

You bug your readers when you describe ANTI-ACID as antacid, suggesting some sort of ant control. You let anti's "i" be dissolved when it met acid. Shame on you. And you really screwed up butterfly, that beautiful and descriptive FLUTTERBY.

* * *

You demonstrate DARING-DO (you call it derring-do) when you foist on us an UNEXPLAINABLE (your inexplicable) preference for words that bear only a passing resemblance to the straight-on ones. All of which DISCOMFORTS me, and probably discomfits you if it bothers you at all.

* * *

HEY WEBSTER...

Your French bias shows when you let your restaurateur stand in for RESTAURANTER and when you give camaraderie billing over the more chummy COMRADERY. And where did you ever find a "helpmeet" to stand in for HELPMATE?

* * *

Why shouldn't your demeanor, which has nothing to do with demeaning, be DEMIENOR since it relates to mien?

* * *

It may not be earth-shaking, but surely TREMBLER is a much better earthquaking word than temblor, which sounds like a water glass. By the way, how can people get tendinitis if they have no tendins? Now admit it, the word should be TENDONITIS

* * *

Your "self-deprecating" should be SELF-DEPRECIATING, shouldn't it? And how can holistic be made whole without your restoring that stolen w to make it WHOLISTIC? You mangled GRAINERY by excising its i and replacing its e with an a to create an abomination: granary. Hey Web, some trimming and grafting is sometimes okay, but let's not get carried away.

* * *

I am CHOMPING (note that I eschew your champing for the more chewable version) at the bit to find the e's you removed from CENTERIST, HINDERANCE, LAUNDERY, and WINTERY to create centrist, hindrance, laundry, and wintry.

* * *

Just a thought: your definition of lackadaisical would best match LAXADAISICAL, which is the accidental coinage by many people, wouldn't it? After all, we're talking lax instead of lack, right?

* * *

You might think I'm being picayune. I disagree. But I might buy PICKYUNE.

NAMEDROPPINGS

Rebellious women!

Why are so many women (or their parents) into name-rebellion? I wouldn't say they're anti-feminine, but their names sure are. For example: Michael Learned, Glenn Close, Sean Young, Sydney Walsh, Jeff Donnell. And Christopher Templeton... why wouldn't her namers at least settle for "Chris?" Why prefer the name in its full form, clearly male, to an abbreviation used by both sexes? Is it an attempt to separate her from Pat and Leslie and other keep-'em-guessing names? (Terri and Teri have solved that problem for Terry.)

* * *

Last-name-firsters also abound: Morgan Fairchild, Whitney Houston, Campbell Brown, Stockard Channing, Harper Lee, and a couple of Taylors: Swift and Caldwell.

* * *

It could be worse: guys named Nancy... or Babette... or Ann... or Elizabeth... or Lili. We're a long way from that point, aren't we?

Ventures in the palin (no, not Sarah) drome

If you asked "What former presidential advisor's name is a palindrome?" and I answered "Sununu's," would I be truthful? And would "a Toyota" be the answer to "Name a palindromic car?"

* * *

Your relatives are a bunch of palindromes: mom (and ma'am), dad, pop, pap, and your sis the nun. Oh yes, and Pip the pup. Plus your cousins Bob, Nan, Otto, Ava, Asa, Ada, Eve, Lil, Gig, and Anna.

* * *

Here's an all-sports palindrome lineup (feel free to recruit more): Football's John Hannah, Jim Otto, Mike Baab, Dennis Harrah, and John Reger. Baseball's Toby Harrah and Mark Salas. Tennis' Monica Seles. Boxing's Willie Pep. And the long-name champion, Russian ice skater Maria Anissina.

* * *

Otto and Baab have another distinction—their names can be turned inside out to form a verb and a singing group: toot and Abba. Finally, "Dennis Harrah sinned" may not result in a criminal sentence, but it is a palindromic one.

Are you a plural person?

Is your last name Phillips, Roberts, Adams, Daniels, Richards, Andrews, Rogers, or Williams? If so, how did you become a plural? Does the "s" change all those first names to last names, and from one person to a clan? If the "s" is simply a possessive which lost its apostrophe, that would explain William Pitt's Pittsburgh (Pitt's-burgh) if not William Penn's Pennsylvania (Penn-sylvania).

* * *

How come there's no Ame, Yate, Holme, Dobb, Rigg, Simmon, Nichol, Picken, or Pott? And how can you keep up with the Joneses if you can't find a single Jone?

NICE (AND OTHERWISE) SOUNDS

Some words just sound nice. Quite apart from their meaning or significance as words, they have a certain lilt, bounce, or smoothness—often due to syllabic cadence or harmony—that lays easy on the ear. There's another bunch of words that have ugly, harsh, or otherwise yucky sounds, also independent of their meaning, and often involving the letters g, j, k, and p. A third group of words I call "stumblers" are difficult to pronounce or to enunciate easily and clearly.

All this is, of course, one person's opinion, one person's experience. Your lists would no doubt be different. But, just to start some discussions, let's go with these:

The nicest ones

I've settled on these 49, a mixture of proper nouns and other words, listed in number-of-syllables order. I found it impossible to list them in a strict order of preference. For some words, it's hard to separate the sound from the images they produce, but I've tried to ignore the meanings and concentrate on the sounds that exit the mouth gracefully. My top selections are in bold face:

REALM ~ ABILINE ~ AVALON ~ CHANDELIER ~ CHEVALIER ~ **DARJEELING** ~ DELILAH ~ **FLEUR-DE-LIS** ~ HEINEKEN ~ ILLUSION ~ MANDALAY ~ NAOMI ~ RENAISSANCE ~ SILHOUETTE ~ SYMPHONY ~ TALULLAH ~ AMARILLO ~

NICE (AND OTHERWISE) SOUNDS

ANACONDA ~ ANEMONE ~ **BENEDICTINE** ~ CATAMARAN ~ CERULEAN ~ DIARRHEA ~ ELYSIAN ~ EVANGELINE ~ **HEINIE MANUSH** ~ HIAWATHA ~ HONOLULU ~ KALAMAZOO ~ MALAGUENA ~ MELANOMA ~ MELLIFLUOUS ~ NEVERTHELESS ~ PERENNIAL ~ PETALUMA ~ PHENOMENON ~ PUSSY WILLOW ~ SERENITY ~ **SHENANDOAH** ~ SOLILOQUY ~ UNANIMOUS ~ BABYLONIA ~ **COPACABANA** ~ LUSITANIA ~ **MONONGAHELA** ~ SANTA MARIA ~ MEGALOMANIA ~ MESOPOTAMIA ~ **BARIUM ENEMA**

The ugliest ones

Again, it's a matter of opinion, of course. And again, it's the sound, not the meaning. Here are my 39, with the "Bottom Ten" (worst) in bold face:

FROG ~ **GAWK** ~ GLITZ ~ GLUB ~ GOOP ~ **GULP** ~ HOOCH ~ JAZZ ~ JUDGE ~ **PLUMP** ~ QUARK ~ **SCREECH** ~ SLUDGE ~ **SPLURGE** ~ BACKTALK ~ BAGHDAD ~ **CATGUT** ~ CHINCH BUG ~ CLOCKWORK ~ **EXCLUDE** ~ GANGPLANK ~ GOBBLE ~ GOOGLE ~ HEDGEHOG ~ HICKOK ~ HODGEPODGE ~ JUKE BOX ~ **MUGWUMP** ~ MUKLUK ~ SQUEEGEE ~ WIGWAG ~ ADJECTIVE ~ KEOKUK ~ **OKMULGEE** ~ INFRASTRUCTURE ~ MADAGASCAR ~ REGURGITATE ~ SKULLDUGGERY ~ **BROBDINGNAGIAN**

And . . . with apologies to the people so-named, I propose forty lashes to all parents who were so unkind as to saddle their newborn with **MAUD(E)**, **DABNEY** (Mr. Coleman, your parents ought to be ashamed of themselves), or **GERTRUDE**—all of which are thankfully rarely bestowed today.

Stumblers

These words trip awkwardly over tongue, lips, palate, and probably teeth on their way to expression. Maybe you can think of more ... and maybe better ones. I've put them in my order of difficulty:

ISTHMUS ~ EIGHTHS ~ THOUSANDTH ~ TSK TSK ~ ANTITHESIS ~ ANESTHETIST ~ ASTHMA ~ OPHTHALMOLOGIST ~ SYNTHESIS ~ STATISTICS ~ LECITHIN ~ RURAL ~ YIELD ~ ULULATE

Some special citations

J. B. White felt that the greatest sound in our language was "the tinkle of ice in a glass at twilight."

* * *

Henry James' two favorite words in the English language: "summer afternoon." Dorothy Parker: "The two most beautiful words are: 'check enclosed.'"

* * *

For me, and for reasons no doubt at least partly rooted in experiences of long ago and in flights of fancy, these words conjure compelling images: Arabian Nights, Cimarron, evensong, nocturne, Vale of Kashmir, shadowlands, summer wind, Song of Hiawatha, twilight, whispering pines, trade winds, Land's End.

Got more?

THE PICKY PART

OF-ALANCHE

On September 5, 2003 I wrote to the Cleveland Plain Dealer as follows:

"Your writers and others are 'of'-ing readers unmercifully:

> '... had found Regina welcoming of their alternative faith ...'

> 'We know the Catholics are very accepting of other religions.'

> '... not supportive of the war.'

> 'Carter is deserving of highest honors ...'

> '... is not likely to be productive of much progress.'

> 'She is fully understanding of ...'

"To pass Journalism 101, you'd use active verbs to say that Regina welcomed, Catholics accept, doesn't support, Carter deserves, not likely to produce, and she fully understands. Active verbs, wimpless writing. Some reminders:

> "The Bible does not say that God was creative of heaven and earth.

"The doctor is not prescriptive of medication.

"We are not told to be preventive of forest fires.

"And you, of all people, should not be screwing up of our language."

A Plain Dealer editor responded:

"I just read your letter about our passive tendencies. I've never enjoyed a complaint letter as much as yours. It made for great reading. Now, the trick is to act on it.

"I share your frustrations with the news writing of today. Writing in the passive voice has become a bad habit. We need to break it. A couple of us here at the Plain Dealer have begun a campaign of sorts to bring back the action verbs. With any luck, you'll witness some successes soon.

"Again, thanks for your letter. It truly made my day."

And it made mine to know that my letter not only was read, but also brought a response of agreement and hope for results. However, a page-wide headline in a later issue of the paper—"Rating isn't always reflective of quality"—is one of many examples that continue the passivity.

Here are more of the invasive "ofs," from various printed sources, that sap the strength of active verbs (in caps) by converting them into passive adverbs:

"... is inclusive of..." INCLUDES

"... is understanding of..." UNDERSTANDS

"... is desirous of..." WANTS

"... to be productive of..." TO PRODUCE

"... is deserving of..." DESERVES

"... is accepting of..." ACCEPTS

"... I am wishing of..." I WISH

"... is violative of..." VIOLATES

"... is respectful of..." RESPECTS

"... they are caring of..." THEY CARE

"... is welcoming of..." WELCOMES

"... is in need of..." NEEDS

"... is admiring of..." ADMIRES

"... was adoring of..." ADORED

"... is appreciative of..." APPRECIATES

"... to be disliking of ..." TO DISLIKE

"... he is condemnatory of ..." HE CONDEMNS

"... I'm wondering of ..." I WONDER

"... If you are suspicious of ..." IF YOU SUSPECT

"... in approval of ..." APPROVE

"... I am of the opinion ..." I BELIEVE

"... is regretful of ..." REGRETS

and the champion contaminator:

"... are supportive of ..." SUPPORT

"Support" is unequivocal, definite, direct. "Supportive of," however, suggests less than full support. It's a "don't quote me" attitude, a wishy-washy stance.

Other culprits of the same ilk:

"... we're in agreement that ..." WE AGREE

"... a few were insistent that ..." A FEW INSISTED

"... we are in opposition ..." WE OPPOSE

"... I'm hopeful that ..." I HOPE

"... it was revealing about ..." IT REVEALED

One final example of the of-alanche, which carries extra baggage of wimpy word waste, is from a newspaper story: "... he is supportive of allowing Ohioans to have ..." Contrast this with this plain and simpler version: "... he wants Ohioans to have ..."

Picky? Yes. But that's what weeds need.

WHEN YOU HAVE THE FLOOR...

If you speak to groups, or on the air, or write for publication, your words take on new power and importance. If one person hears your mispronunciation of nuclear as "nuke you-lur," it's no big deal; informal conversation allows slips. But if a large number of people hear or read it, the error could spread exponentially.

You don't need to pre-edit casual conversations, but you should be aware of meadow muffins as you romp through the language field. Here are some prominent ones:

- There is no mo in MEMENTO. Remember, it's about memory.

- LARYNX is lair-inks, not lar-nicks.

- You HOME in on a target, but you HONE a blade. The words are somewhat similar but not interchangeable.

- Contrary to what you hear all too often, the end of JUDICIARY ("ee-ary") rhymes with incendiary, not the end of Jan-you-ary.

- NEGOTIATE ends in "she ate," not "see ate."

- The o in PERCOLATE doesn't allow perk-you-late.

- The "el" in JEWELRY often gets "le." Jewlery is fake.

- NUPTIAL should be mutual, but the pronunciation favors partial.

- ESCALATE? Yes. Esculate? No. Maybe you're thinking of osculate.

- You may get express service, but your ESPRESSO is x-less.

- ASTERISK has three syllables with a risk, not two with a trick.

- The kyoo-pon you clipped is no good. The COUPON is what you wanted.

- When you pronounce ACCESSORY, avoid the ass. The c's have a k sound. So do the ones in SUCCINCT and the first one in ECSTATIC. If you can't find a k sound, take it out of a non-word in which it doesn't belong . . . "ekcetera," for example.

- Pronounce JUBILANT, VANILLA, and LASSO as they are spelled. That'll keep you from erring with jubulant, vanella, and lassoo.

- "Simular" may owe its mistaken sound to the somewhat SIMILAR "simulate."

- STRENGTH and LENGTH often lose their essential g's and become non-words "strenth" and "lenth."

HEIGHT rhymes with kite, but the tongue-y "-th" can bring it down.

- For those of you who are likely to be around in 2061 when HALLEY'S Comet returns, make a note to rhyme it with galley, not gaily.

- The event can't re-occur. It can, however, RECUR. I don't know why the "oc" left.

- A bull in a china shop is a one-animal wrecking crew, but the havoc that results is WREAKED—a freaky word that has staked a legitimate claim, even though "wrecked" is more descriptive.

- "Supposably" and "undoubtably" are trying to ably masquerade as SUPPOSEDLY and UNDOUBTEDLY. I hope you will not allow this deception.

- Jerry and jury and rigged and built are constantly running into each other. With good reason. JURY-RIGGED (not necessary similar to a rigged jury) describes a makeshift something-or-other. If it's JERRY-BUILT, it's a cheap and flimsy thing put together hastily. So what's the difference? Not much that I can see. Like resin/rosin and egoism/egotism, the differences aren't great.

- Don't feel deficient if you have to resort to the dictionary for proper pronunciation. Like you, I often go to Webster's—to be reminded that ERR is pronounced both ur (first choice) and air, that AVER is uh-'ver (second syllable emphasis), and that IGNO-MINY has first-syllable emphasis, although the third syllable of IGNOMINIOUS is the stressed one.

- An ORANGUTAN doesn't have a tail, so you shouldn't try to graft a g onto its end.

TROUBLEMAKERS

The GROUND is hereby grounded because of its efforts to impersonate legitimacy. The evidence is in these newspaper stories:

> *Wrestling:* "I was surprised he called it a pin, because his shoulders were four inches off the ground."
>
> *Boxing:* "The referee stepped in to stop Lesnar from pummeling Mir to the ground."
>
> *Fitness class:* "He scoped out the gym and . . . placed a duffel bag on the ground . . . ."
>
> *Basketball game*: ". . . grabbed his neck after the hard foul and lay on the ground for several minutes . . . ."
>
> *On a school bus:* ". . . was shoved to the ground."

The facts: Wrestlers and boxers perform on mats. If you fall in a gym, an arena, or a school bus, you fall to the floor. Come to think of it, what are you doing on a school bus at your age?

3W overload—WORDY, WIMPY, WASTEFUL:

> When the TV weatherman said, "The weather in Atlanta at this particular point in time is clear," instead

of "Our weather is clear," he missed an opportunity to get to the point eight words (and 13 syllables) faster. However, air time between commercials must be filled, so unnecessary words are often enlisted.

"... the season could end with six unbeaten teams, though obviously that probably won't happen." Good old *obviously/probably* and sometimes a *definitely/maybe* lets reporters, writers, and pundits have it both ways to avoid commitment.

"I'm just sort of like maybe if I didn't see any of it, I'll be fine." The sentence could have boasted near-total degradation if a "y'know" and a "whatever' could have been slipped in somehow.

"... signaled that he would have liked to have had more evidence ... ." That's a cumbersome way to say "he wanted more evidence." But the judge was speaking, not writing, and sometimes a rushed interview allows no time to pause and compose crisper thoughts as a writer would do. So let's not indict him.

"They didn't necessarily go to church often." What is lost if "necessarily" is removed? Nothing. The word is not necessary here.

T. I. C. GRAMMAR RULES

With Tongue In Cheek I offer these rules, gathered from numerous sages.

1. Be more or less specific.

2. Make each pronoun agree with their antecedents.

3. Don't use Capital letters without a good reason.

4. I've told you a thousand times to resist hyperbole.

5. Write all adverbial forms correct.

6. It behooves us to avoid archaisms.

7. Avoid commas, that are not necessary.

8. The passive voice should be avoided.

9. The rigid rule of "i before e except after c" raises spelling to a sceince.

10. Never, ever use repetitive redundancies.

11. Proofread your writing to see if you any words out.

12. Don't verb nouns.

13. Take the bull by the hand and don't mix metaphors.

T. I. C. GRAMMAR RULES

14. Use parallel structure when you write and in speaking.

15. Boycott eponyms.

16. About those sentence fragments.

17. Who needs rhetorical questions?

18. Just between you and I, case is important too.

19. Don't write run-on sentences they are hard to read.

20. Correct speling is essential.

21. Don't use no double negatives.

22. Ixnay on colloquial stuff.

23. Never use a long word where a diminutive one will do.

24. Last but not least, avoid cliches like the plague.

WANT TO PLAY EDITOR?

This little essay is a good test for you if you'd like to go into journalism or want to be a writer. I've adapted it from the original version which came from Merritt Johnquest. Suggestion: copy it for your friends and compare your editing skills; you'll probably find it easy to spot their misses and mistakes. There is no one perfect score, and there is more than one right answer in a few cases. But use a pencil; ink is hard to erase.

Proper english usage is a very important skill to develop, irregardless of profession. When one misuses the language, it can have a negative effect on you. There's nothing more irritating than a writer who constantly makes the same mistakes over and over again. More importantly, its the the kind of thing that can wreck havoc on your credibility.

Just between you and I, this copy has several errors on it that are violative of good writing-spelling, punctuation, grammer, incorrect word choice, syntax, or word order in

119

this document, your job is to find them.

Some of them may be difficult to identify: others are as easy as falling off a piece of cake. Undoubtably, you won't find where all of them are at. Neither you nor myself are that profficient.

And that's okay. You won't be graded on this rather unique quiz. Its different than others. There are no free gifts.

We want only you to try your best To learn a lot and enjoy yourself in the process.

Sheldon Harper is a West Virginia Ohioan. He was born in 1921 in Frenchton, West Virginia, and schooled in Fairmont, West Virginia, graduating from East Fairmont High in 1939. He moved to Akron, Ohio in 1939, graduated from Hammel Business University there in 1940, and worked at Goodyear Aircraft Corporation before World War II military service from 1942-46. At Ohio State University he received a BA degree in journalism in 1950 and edited the campus daily, *The Lantern*, in his senior year.

Father of four, grandfather of seven, and widowed since 2000, his marriage to Juanita Glisson in 1948 endured for more than 51 years. Currently he lives in Strongsville, Ohio, with Madge (Claudia) Lee.

He has been an advertising manager and writer for Goodyear Tire & Rubber Company in Akron, Berkley & Company in Iowa, and, in Cleveland, True Temper Corporation, Mills Hall Walborn advertising agency, and Cuyahoga Savings.

He has been a reporter/writer for city publications in Brecksville and Broadview Heights, both in Ohio, and a councilman in the latter city.

He has been writing a newsletter, now numbering 67 issues since 1989, to his high school classmates.

Because he has been writing for many years, and because he has been away from the nine-to-five life since 1986, he can reasonably be called a has-been.

I am Sheldon Harper and I approve this message.

Publisher:

Harper Ink
17322 Otani Ct.
Strongsville, OH 44136

Email: harperinkpress@gmail.com